Rabia's Return

"Rabia's Return" (Rabia'nın Dönüşü)
Translated by Figen Bingöl
State University of New York, Purchase Collage

"Defend My Love You Defend" (Savun Sevdam Savun)
Translated by Nilüfer Mizanoğlu-Reddy
Twenty Stories by Turkish Women Writers.
Indiana University Turkish Studies, 1988

Edited by Tanju Anapa

Design Consultant Bülent Erkmen, BEK
Cover design by Yetkin Başarır, BEK

1 st Edition, April 2005

ISBN: 975 331 729-8

Publisher:
Epsilon Yayıncılık Hizmetleri Tic. San. Ltd. Şti.
Osmanlı Sk. 24/4 80090 Taksim/İstanbul
Tel: 0212 252 38 21 pbx Faks: 0212 252 47 29
www.epsilonyayinevi.com
e-mail: epsilon@epsilonyayinevi.com

Printed by Melisa Matbaası
Çiftehavuzlar Yolu Acar Sitesi No:4 Davutpaşa / İstanbul
Tel: 0212 480 07 75

Distributor:
Yeni Çizgi Yayın Dağıtım Ltd. Şti.
Gürsel Mah. Alaybey Sk. No: 7
Kağıthane/İstanbul
Tel: 0212 220 57 70 pbx Faks: 0212 222 61 55
Online orders: www.yenisayfa.com

Adalet Ağaoğlu

Born in 1929 in Nallihan near Ankara, Adalet Ağaoğlu studied French at Ankara University and joined in drama department of Ankara Radio. During the Fifties, Sixties and Seventies, she achieved prominence as a playwright, writing for various theatres, especially for the Ankara State during its heyday. In the early Seventies, she began writing novels. "A Wedding Night" (1979) won all the main Turkish literary awards. Since then, she has established herself as one of the leading writers of Turkey. Ağaoğlu firmly rejects being labeled as a female or feminist writer, preferring to be known simply as a "writer".

"Curfew" was published in 1984 and forms one part of a highly successful triptych concerning Eighties. Her latest novel, "Romance/A Viennese Novel" came out to acclaim in October 1993. Her latest play, "Too Near and Yet Too Far" was performed in 1993/94 by Kent Players, a prominent theater group of Turkey.

In December 1995, Ağaoğlu received Turkish Presidential Award of Merit for her services to art and culture, and in 1997, she received the prestigious Aydın Doğan Foundation Prize for Literature for "Romantic".

Adalet Ağaoğlu lives in Istanbul.

Rabia's Return

Translated by Figen Bingöl

Defend My Love You Defend

Translated by Nilüfer Mizanoğlu Reddy

epsilon®

Contents

Foreword for "Rabia's Return"

Adalet Ağaoğlu's short story "Rabia's Return" holds within it another story, which is taken from one of the most popular novels in Turkish literature. This novel was initially written by Halide Edip Adıvar in English with the title *The Clown and His Daughter*. It was published in London in 1935. Later, in 1936, it was published in Turkish with the title *Sinekli Bakkal* (The Fly-filled Grocery), and became a bestseller of the time.

Halide Edip Adıvar (1884-1964), the first important woman writer in Turkey, started her literary career in early 1920s. She published eighteen novels, many short stories, plays and translations. Nilüfer Mizanoğlu Reddy notes that Adıvar "discovered her vocation as a writer during the constitutional reform movement of 1908 by the Young Turks. She was involved in the events of 1908 to 1922, a period of wars and revolutions, both as an activist and author." She was one of the major contributors to Mustafa Kemal's movement towards the establishment of a new Turkey. She also wrote about women's emancipation.

Adıvar's novel portrays a poor neighborhood in İstanbul at the time of the Ottoman Sultan Abdülhamid II (1876-1909). The protagonist Rabia is a strong-minded woman from this neighborhood who is a reciter of the Koran. The novel deals with the times' social and political issues through the depiction of characters from different classes.

Emine is the daughter of the imam (leader of the Muslim congregation) of the neighborhood. She marries Tevfik, the actor and the owner of the fly-filled grocery store, against her father's will. Tevfik is called 'Girl Tevfik' in the neighborhood because he plays the part of a woman in a local type of drama called 'orta oyunu'. Emine cannot get along with her husband and comes back to the house of her very traditional and fanatically religious father. Meanwhile Tevfik becomes a very famous actor. Then he is exiled from İstanbul for impersonating a woman in one of his plays.

Emine bears Tevfik's child; they name the baby girl Rabia. She is raised by her grandfather in a very strict, religious way. He has Rabia memorize the Koran and she becomes a person who chants prayers on occasions such as weddings, funerals, etc. Rabia is under the protection of Selim Pasha, a cabinet member, and his wife. Rabia has an extraordinarily beautiful voice and becomes very famous in İstanbul. Grandpa Vehbi, a Sufi dervish whose philosophy of life consists of tolerance, universality and peace as the face of the Islamic world, teaches Rabia Turkish classical music in the Pasha's mansion. Then the Italian music teacher Peregrini, who comes to the mansion to give piano lessons to the Pasha's son, meets Rabia and falls in love with her.

When Rabia is about ten years old, Tevfik returns from exile and again opens the grocery store. Rabia leaves her mother and grandfather and starts living with her father. Soon after her departure, Emine dies.

In those times, an underground group called the 'Young Turks' was working against the Sultan and the regime. Selim Pasha's son is one of them and Pasha is aware of this, but he has no tolerance for those against the regime, including his son. Tevfik, to help the Young Turks, dresses up as a woman and picks up their publications coming in from Europe at a French post office. In the process, he gets arrested. Pasha does not prevent his son and Tevfik from being exiled.

Thus, Rabia, who has become very attached to her father is left all alone. She takes over the grocery store and earns additional money by chanting prayers.

Peregrini, in order to be able to marry Rabia, converts to islam and changes his name to Osman. Even though he is a wealthy man and is accustomed to living in mansions, he agrees to live in the fly-fîlled neighborhood for Rabia's consent. He is quite a bit older than Rabia, is raised in Western ways, and also comes from a different class. These differences cause conflicts between him and Rabia. But Rabia is strong-minded and never compromises the Eastern values originating from her religion, culture and class. The main clash between them becomes clear when Peregrini wants to move to a bigger place; however Rabia does not leave the neighborhood. In the midst of their conflict. Rabia's grandfather, the imam passes away. Rabia and Osman settle in the imam's house, which is a bigger house, but still in the same neighborhood. In a way, this is a compromise between them by which Peregrini finds space and privacy for his studies on writing an opera. There, Rabia gives birth to a baby boy.

Meanwhile, Selim Pasha, who used to be loyal to the Sultan, changes his views and leaves his post. He now regrets being so strict towards his son and the other Young Turks. After the declaration of the Constitutional Monarchy (1908), Tevfik returns from exile and he is greeted like a hero. The times have changed and all the conflicts are resolved. Tevfik reunites with his daughter and grandson and the novel ends happily.

The novel portrays the conflicts between the cultures of East and West, yet at the end it finds a reconciliation between them. Rabia and Peregrini's baby, indeed, is the symbol of the new Turk coming out of this union. The author Selim İleri in his commentary on the novel, suggests that the novel emphasizes the transmission of cultural, artistic and traditional values from past to present during the times of change. The novel searches for the role of the East in the midst of westernization. Rabia is at peace with the conservative customs; however she loves Peregrini. Even though Peregrini becomes Osman, he does not abandon his own music. İleri remarks that the East-West clash soothes through art and culture is resolved in the novel. The Eastern and Western cultures supplement each other; the absence of either one would be the end of the fly-filled neighborhood's happiness.

Adalet Ağaoğlu revisits this story in 'Rabia's Return', published in 1997, which questions the happy ending of the novel. The narrator of Ağaoğlu's story is a woman of our times, who lives in modern İstanbul and is one of the many readers of the *Clown and His Daughter*. She looks at the past through Rabia's character and questions the place of woman in today's society, which has ostensibly been modernized.

The story is full of references to the novel, as well as some other classics in Turkish literature, and it is not very clear who the narrator is. Sometimes she talks as if she lives in the times of the novel: For instance she talks about the dervish Vehbi as "the Grandpa Vehbi of all of us," or refers to the crowd who are greeting those coming from exile as "we". These kinds of shifts between the subjects of then and now are Ağaoğlu's way of relating the reader to the novel itself. The novel has been so well known to Turkish readers that they almost feel themselves as one of the characters in it. At the same time, Ağaoğlu gives many hints that the narrator lives at the present time. There are numerous contemporary references to her airplane trip, the bombs used by anarchists in the 1970's, the high-rise hotel roofs, the dinner cruises along the Bosphorus, etc.

The narrator, as a reader of the novel, thinks about what could have happened after the actual ending, which is Tevfik's return from exile in the novel. The narrator goes beyond the novel and creates a new story and reveals the haunting memory of Rabia in her own life. Rabia is a figure that belongs to past; however she is still alive in our day with her traditional role. Even though the narrator lives in a modern society, there are the residues and remnants of the past everywhere. The past and present are intertwined in the story to emphasize what has been changed in the name of modernization, and what has not. The woman's place and status today are reminiscent of those in the time of Rabia. In these terms, Rabia has never gone. It's a shadow following today's woman wherever she goes.

Figen Bingöl

Works Cited

İleri, Selim. "*Sinekli Bakkalca.* Son Satırlar" (The Last Lines for The Clown and His Daughter). *Sinekli Bakkal* (The Clown and His Daughter). İstanbul: Özgür Yayinları, 1999.

Rabia's Return

Rabia is back, they said.

In voices full of worry: Rabia is back...

Had she ever gone away somewhere? Where to? We had forgotten about her.

As if the news of Rabia's return has made everyone more friendly, even those who had been lifelong-hidden-enemies. I got the feeling that everybody, especially women, had established a quick solidarity and wanted to build an unyielding wall against the person whose return they considered a disaster. Just a few minutes ago I mean, at the dinner party I was invited to. The mood of a kind of horror, more than that of a worry, disturbed me. I asked the host's permission with the excuse of a headache, and left the gathering early.

It wasn't really a lie. Thanks to the two small glasses of wine I had at dinner, my mouth was sticky, I felt a heavy load on my head, a kind of blurriness.

I did not want to go home right away. I went down and started to walk right around here, on the shores of the Bosphorous which happens to be very quiet at this season, with very little illumination at night.

I cannot see well in front of me. I walk slowly. I feel safe in the canal formed by the large tree-trunks on the land and the sea on the other side. More ahead. The mixed smell of fried fish, rakı*, and smoke, billowing from the fish restaurants near the village of Bosphorus, interweaves into the texture of night as if it fuses into a coarse woven dark colored fabric. Yet I know: a little later, the northwest wind will pick up, this smell will leave its place to the mixed smell of wet leaves, seaweed, iodine; and even the thickest smoke, the stickiest humidity will flow right away like the rain drops hitting a slippery surface; the night will glitter with its natural darkness.

Rabia's voice was said to be God-given. Maybe, maybe not.

At the dinner to which I was invited, there were friends, acquaintances whom I hadn't seen for a long time. I knew that one of them had married a

* An anise flavored liquor made from grape juice.

Frenchman years ago. They lived in her husband's country for a while, but later on my friend started to whine, I am nothing in these places, I cannot feel myself settled, ah my country, and returned. But since she wasn't divorced, she did not consider herself "returned". She herself said so, with a carefree laugh. Whatever she feels like, half there, half here... Their children were studying in the USA There was also another friend of mine who was married to a Norwegian lady, an archaelogist. The archaelogist was working here in Turkey; they met then and got married. Afterwards, they stayed here for good, visiting Norway from time to time —at Christmas times and so on... My friend's wife says she can't have enough of the sun and the sea in this country. Their children were educated in England; each one of them had married someone from a different part of the world. Nothing like the days when the news of Rabia's marriage had caused such commotion... Our host works as representatives of a British news agency and the hostess, his wife is Turkish. I met her tonight. I gather she is teaching Art History classes at a university. I knew the English husband beforehand but I didn't know that he attended church every Sunday. He did, in fact, taking along his Turkish wife. The Art Historian laughed when she said this, and added: "Actually I have nothing to do either with my own religion, or with another one, but I go, you see..." Considering the common element in their marriages, it is not that difficult, in a way, to understand why they were so interested in Rabia's return. Rabia had made abreach in the obstacle to the union of a man and a woman who come from two different societies such as East and West, especially from two different religions – and this, in a conservative family like hers, in a conservative circle. If such an introverted Rabia from a highly traditional neighborhood was proposed to by a foreign man and married to him, it only meant that a very strict prohibition in this area has got a hole in its very foundation. In other words, Rabia has been a pioneer of Muslim-Christian marriages. Moreover, her marriage is the 'happy ending' symbol of the union of two cultures. For many years it was known as such. It was that 'happy ending' light that was looked up to in all steps that were taken and would still be taken on this path. To the extent that this kind of marriages became natural and the symbol –ei. "happy ending" ceased to be a symbol and was forgotten all together... Now we live in a time where many white-horsed princes and many daughters of fairytale-sultans live happily ever after. But, right now, dark shadows are falling onto the first known 'happy ending': Rabia has returned...

The man she married... A-ha, of course, "was the son of a Spanish nobleman. He was born in Madrid, grew up there. He did not know his father, his mother raised him. A man taking many shapes among opposing desires from the beginning till the end" so he was. He used to tell Grandpa Vehbi that his mother ruined him both with her religion and her excessive love. He wanted to study music in Milan; his mother, too, went with him. She sold their mansion in Madrid; she changed her nationality and became an Italian because the Pope was Italian. Of course, she made her son change his nationality too... She spent all they had for the benefit of the Catholic Church. Italian Peregrini. He was giving piano lessons to the children of rich in Istanbul. Fell in love with the beautiful-voiced Rabia.

Is Rabia's return a mirror held to the faces of those who could not find what they expected from the union of the different worlds? Is that the reason for this uneasiness?

This, too, comes to my mind: None of the marriages that followed Rabia's has involved a change of religion on the part of men. If anyone changed, it was generally the women who changed their names and religions. Maybe because of this. Rabia's ability to attract men planted a seed of jealousy in the others, without their knowledge. Maybe that's the reason why they feel discomfort even at the mention of Rabia's name.

Rabia, the one whose never smiling face bloomed as a rose only at the sight of the piano teacher in front of the grocery store or at upper class people's houses that she was called into because of her beautiful voice... How long had it been anyway since she got together again with her father after a fatherless childhood? Now, this time that father was exiled from the country. But, meanwhile in this neighborhood with the fly-filled grocery store, Rabia has already filled the vacuum of the love epic left by Emine and Tevfik with the fire of ' Osman the Italian,' only burning more furiously. But with a big difference: Except for Grandpa Vehbi of all of us, who calls upon everybody to be merciful, it does not look likely that anybody will yield to Osman or tolerate him. And Rabia is under a continuous eye-and-ear surveillance. The piano teacher had even changed his religion for the girl, as well as his name! Just because he did so, Rabia?.. No, no. Rabia keeps saying that marriage is not possible, even if his name is Osman, even if he's become a Muslim. Ah, that's what you think; if she finds encouragement in the neighborhood, she will slip into the bed of the infidel right away! How lively her voice became, aren't you aware? My dear, do you think, like her ma' she will grab her knapsack and go to the man?.. Yours are empty words; the poor girl is saying, they will think I would be marrying him for the money, I will earn my own bread myself until the end of my life, even though my father is exiled, I will run the grocery store; and she does what she says, look at her! Also, there is what she earned with her God given voice... Neither hungry, nor naked; why would she marry a foreigner? That is true, I, too. heard from the woman who cleans the Headmaster's house, when they told Rabia about the entertainer-teacher's proposal, she had raised her head with an attitude and said: I don't need a helping hand from a foreigner, sir. I don't believe it. If Rabia has loved two living beings on this earth until today, one is her father Tevfik, the other one is this man. You'll see...

She has returned.

Little Rabia$_S$ whose mysterious voice fills souls deeply... Her sad face, her eyes full of mystery looking not at this world only, but at the after-life... Years later, only these are in my thoughts now. What is vibrating in the dimness of the Bosphorus night is that voice again. If it wasn't for her voice, Rabia could have been considered to be completely non-existent. However, because of that voice, she would be subject to all kinds of comments, wherever she turned that sad face. But, what was her life about anyway? In the narrow space between a fly-filled grocery store, which gave the neighborhood its name, and the house of a conservative grandfather who never knew anything of joy, of pleasing someone, or of love, she lived as if she had really turned her back on this earth. Moreover, as if she had to keep her head down, because of her mother's eloping with the grocery storeowner's actor son...

I see Rabia now again in her little girl image. She is coming out of the İlhami Efendi* Mansion, where she had taken refuge with her mother, at the age of only eight, her head covered with a scarf, wearing a faded dress coming all the way down to her ankles, filling her water jug at the shadowy fountain of the neighborhood. Healing water for her grandpa. And the jug is so big compared to the poor child's size! We simply forgot that she had never been allowed to be a child, she had never known a father's secure lap; or maybe we pretended to forget. A few caring people used to say: the girl's voice is so melancholic because she cannot cry, she bottles up everything inside because she doesn't cry. At weddings, circumcision ceremonies. and funerals, everyone who hired her to chant a few

* A title traditionally used after the names of high-ranking members of Ottoman society.

pieces, a few prayers, used to be mesmerized by that voice.

Hadji* İlhami Efendi, was keeping his granddaughter under strict control since he was devastated by his daughter's adventure with Tevfik. Well, he had restricted Emine too; what good did it do? Emine had been asked to stay away from any kind of love affair whatsoever, but you see, she had fallen in love with the actor son of the grocery storeowner. And Tevfik had been waiting for her at street corners. Emine and Tevfik. No September has ever seen such a fire. Back then, around here, the love affairs in these Bosphorus villages could never have been as brave as the ones in the other neighborhoods. No other heart fire had exposed itself so openly. For instance, Suad — she did not grab her bag and run away to Necip; Necip was not brave enough to whisk Suad away in a boat. Well, Necip's wind was not so powerful to stir up dreams of sailing at full speed, or to make the roofs and chimneys fly, anyway. "Love affairs for one summer" that is what they are. Emine on the other hand threw herself into Tevfik's arms even though she knew her father would not 'give his daughter to a poor excuse for an actor.' Because Tevfik was Tevfik. Since his childhood,

* A title used for a Muslim pilgrim who visits Mecca in Saudi Arabia for religious reasons.

he was humorous, 'long-legged, strong, his chestnut eyes sweet as a girl's, his red lips talking without ever stopping, naughty, a clown boy...' Everybody found him lighthearted but Tevfik had every 'God given' quality of a folk artist. If needed, he would even dress like a woman, jump on the stage, tell everything that everybody wouldn't say but wanted to hear about the rulers, satirize them, and steal the hearts of everybody, man or woman. A man such as Tevfik falls for Emine and Emine says no... Not possible! Yet, the same Emine, by the same neighborhood's saying, 'had got what was coming to her.' She had come to realize that it was not possible to settle down with an irresponsible, flighty man, all play and acting, she had returned to her father's home like an exhausted warrior. What remained from the Emıne-Tevfık epic, which ended with a failed dream, was a child. Upon returning to her hadji father's home, Emine was pregnant with Rabia... Hadji İlhami Efendi, on the other hand, was almost paralized with a breakdown, but what could he do, a female child, he can neither sell nor store... He took Emine in, closed the doors, windows. He forbade the actor to see his newborn daughter. Only when his daughter goes to the grave like himself will the master of mercy, Grandpa Vehbi, allow Rabia to embrace her father. They say Rabia couldn't shed one tear even then!... Always bottled up everything inside... She had been like that since the day the loveless grandfather had thrown her doll into the fire and burnt it. She had so many tears that she could not shed. That's why her voice resonated from so deep, and was so volumed.

Rabia has returned...

I wonder, if her voice is still that muffled, that moving?

The Bosphorus breeze has not picked up yet. What makes me tired is not that past, but this humid air. In fact, how many steps have I taken in the past that I should be so tired?

People always wish to see the house where they were born in, to walk once more through the childhood, the adolescent days. On the days that I settled down around here, first thing I also did was to go and see the places on the Bosphorus where Suad, Süreyya and Necip, whose other names to me were 'The Fallen Leaves of September' lived and strolled. Because back then, I too, had watched them for the whole summer. Suad and Süreyya. The young married couple. Necip. Their family friend, flighty youth. But his acting is only attuned to love affairs. The young couple had wanted to spend a summer away from the mansion where they lived with their elders, far from their imprisoning eyes, and had rented a waterfront house on the Bosphorus. Of course, the one who found the house for them was Necip who knew the answers to each and every what, where and when. I went to look for that waterfront house. The summer when Suad fell in love with Necip in a dream of freedom. Necip's seasonal love, which he lived this time around in the 'impossible.' Suad, a flower in a vase for both of the men. Waiting to be picked and smelled... At the end, the waterfront house, rented for a single summer, had burnt and turned to ashes along with those who had dived into the dream of freedom.

Back then, we knew every neighborhood of the city, whatever had been experienced in each. Lives would open in front of our eyes like the pages of a novel one by one, and then pass, dragging.

I am not sure if at one point I heard that the burnt waterfront house was sold by the owners, with the idea that it was burned down because it was sinfull and was rebuilt true to its original form by a stranger or I made this all up, somehow, I thought the waterfront house was standing there like a flaming love torch. On the other hand, forgot where the house was located, I couldn't recognize the area, I couldn't even remember where it was. What remains from that September of fire is again the flowing waters, again that whirlpool...

Now, people lament for the past constantly; they yearn for the past for its waterfront houses, its love affairs, but on the condition that they who were burned yesterday would stay where they were burned and that they would not come back to interfere with our lives today. Probably what bothered me the most at the dinner was this air covering me all over. May the lives be forgotten, the wooden mansions and waterfront houses be ours.

Rabia has returned.

What I heard last about her is that she didn't want the mansion, which had been left deserted after her mother's and grandfather's deaths, to be rented. That she settled there with her husband Osman. Of course she married 'Italian Osman'; Grandpa Vehbi's philosophy of mercy was helpful both for the two of them and for everybody else. The rumor is that some invisible hand was helping Grandpa Vehbi, but I only believe in the magic and spell of novels, not of real life. Therefore, now, in this darkness I keep asking: Why would Rabia leave the old mansion that she settled in with so much fervor? Where would she have gone away from this house where she welcommed her father's return from exile that she would return?

My friends, my acquaintances at the dinner probably were taking the news of Rabia's return not only with worry or hostility; they were also looking down on her. Both fear and contempt. How strange! So what if Rabia has returned? What's the use of sighing, of hollow stubbornness, if you can't change the direction of life and prevent the inevitable? Other than to add a few more to the storm-broken branches?

Just as I was thinking of all that, the breeze picked up.

The winter nights on the Bosphorus get brighter than those in summer. In summer, the Black Sea wind carries humidity, and haze settles down. The north-west wind, on the other hand, loads the haze on its back, drags it away. The current of the water and the current of the air at such times join in a soft harmony. At the moment, the current on the surface is sliding downwards hand in hand with the wind. Partly cloudy up above, wings of seagulls perched upon the same sled. Down under in the deep, however, the whirlpool, again that whirlpool...

I snuggle in my coat. The cool air hitting my fore-head puts me in a state of drunkenness – something wine couldn't achieve. Even the faded, wide and shal-low lights at this side of the shore are growing, getting bigger as they reflect on the water. I can see where I am going only with the help of the light reflected on the water.

A little ways away from me, two boats are passing, back-to-back, decorated with colorful light bulbs lined up on the cables stretched between their poles and rails. They are the floating restaurants of hotels or the pubs of the *nouveau riche* who had the water carry their pubs on its shoulders... The boats with these colorfully lit triangles stretched between the sea and the sky resemble a Karagöz* hut in the Karagöz plays. Girl Tevfik. With his jokes, he used to bring cheer even to his sullen uncle's grocery store, that dusty place full of flies. Actor Tevfik. It's him again, you see. It's Tevfik who puts up the curtain, lights the lantern, makes the neighborhood people act in Karagöz plays, and plays the woman's part in the imitated 'ortaoyunu.'** Later on, he had become a famous cabaret actor who satirized politicians with more poisonous arrows. This famous actor seen and known by everybody and now became "the voice of the people" has not been seen by her daughter only. Rabia. She has returned.

Years passed. Then, we... Well actually the reason why he was sentenced to live in exile was the fact that he disguised himself as a woman. Later on, we greet-

---

* A Punch-and-Judy style shadow show that was popular at the turn of the 20th Century.

** A theatrical genre based on story telling and improvisation once popular in Turkey.

ed Tevfik Bey* -now that was the way to call him- at the Galata Port when he returned from exile thanks to the amnesty.** We. The ones who follow the whole adventure like reading a novel page by page on comfortable couches. Tevfik Bey is a symbol of freedom now. The times have changed; he was greeted as such. Hero of freedom. But he was old and tired. Rabia's husband. 'Italian Osman,' as we came to call him now, was at the quay. And everybody's Grandpa Vehbi was at the quay. But more importantly, that big crowd. That big crowd that we did not recognize, whose affiliation we did not know, as if wanting to celebrate a freedom festival like this for once, filled the port, all were applauding those who made it to their homeland after so many years of longing...

Westernize the regime. The people in exile were pardoned and came back..

Rabia's voice, again with that full, deep, penetrating tone takes over the crowd's humming. But now this voice is not that of little Rabia, who has always hidden herself behind her voice, but the voice of a young woman who besieged the world not only with her emotions but with her rationality as well. This new

---

* A title meaning Mr. (used after a first name).

** Amnesty after the declaration of the Constitutional Monarchy in 1908, a movement in the Ottoman Empire to

picture has been standing just like that in my memory for quite a long time. Since that day of welcome: The voice of a lullaby-singing young mother. The voice of a breastfeeding young mother. The voice wearing out the husband more and more...

Among those greeting Tevfik Bey at the port was also the 'Eye Punching Muzaffer' of the sad days that are finally left behind not only for Rabia, but also for her father. Tevfik Bey, who suddenly saw Muzaffer while preaching praises for those coming back from exile, had gotten very upset. Everything about that scene is in front of my eyes as if it all happened yesterday. He had asked his son-in-law Osman: "What's this man doing here?"" Before being sent to exile, when he was under many kinds of torture in prison 'the hands that made thousands of stars fly' in front of his eyes and the hands that kept echoing in his ears even at that moment were the same short fingered, broad, hairy hands which now Muzaffer was holding out, pointing to Tevfik Bey, roaring to the welcoming crowd "Heyyy, you lover of freedom and equality, I will strangle whoever attempts to go against this revolution and its founders, with these very hands." His son-in-law, holding his arm, pulling him to the side, wanted to take his father-in-law away from the frustration at his first moment; I heard him say, "Come on, let's get away from this crowd." Tevfik Bey's eyes were looking for someone among the people applauding, waving hats, and handkerchiefs; not being able to bear it any more he asked: "Where's Rabia?"

Rabia has returned, they said...

Ahh, but the only person whose return I can see, on this deserted, dim Bosphorus night, is Tevfik Bey. Where's Rabia?

"Rabia is dolling up that grandson of yours. Mother and son, they're waiting for the hero of our neighborhood."

It was Grandpa Vehbi who said this. His eyes were wet: O c'est la vie! Easier said than done. Just when you were united with your child, you go and get arrested in woman's clothes while mailing the organization's manifestoes against the government from the post office... You all went away young, came back old.

Meanwhile Tevfik Bey made a moaning sound saying, "Grandson... Grandson...," I remember very well. His eyes, too, got wet, also all of ours... Grandpa Vehbi, this smiling face of all times, to cheer up this incredibly sad atmosphere of welcome-reunion, moving the back of his hands in front of his eyes hastily, teased: "You now add a child to the dream team, Tevfik." We all laughed.

The sky cleared.

The sorrows released.

Tevfik Bey quickened his step to see his grandson as soon as possible. Grandpa Vehbi, in his youth, used to mistakenly call the cabaret theater group that 'Girl Tevfik' had assembled, the Dream Team, taken from the Karagöz-Ortaoyunu shows that he had performed as a child... True, the master of satire of long ago days had not added a child to his group. Was it because of Rabia, who had been born in her grandfather's house without a father, that he felt guilty about children? Or was it a result of escaping from daily responsibilities, not being able to care of them, while he pursued big goals? This question comes to my mind now.

Now they were getting into the cars. I left them at this point.

Tevfik Bey, what did he do and how did he feel at the times when he saw Rabia singing lullabies to his grandson always with the same, deep, melancholic voice? What happened to them later? I heard that he did or that he would assemble a new group, but I read in the newspaper they gave out on the airplane while returning from a trip that he was found dead at his house. It's as if a big, very deep hole was opened in me. God forbid, did he die alone, all alone? Anyway, later, had the convert-from-Christianity-to-Islam Osman taken Rabia and her child to his country? Who knows, maybe they settled down there for good. After all, how many families were left in the city to take private lessons from a piano teacher?

It was Rabia who wanted to settle in the Grandpa İmam* Mansion after their marriage. Those well acquainted with them know this. Right after they got married, she insisted on living in that old wooden house -just as she had insisted before. "I run the grocery store, I earn my living myself." I haven't seen it, but who knows how beautifully the 'Italian Osman', feeling that he entered the mysterious world of the East, believing that he had reached the pinnacle, had that old house fixed up for Rabia! Probably, he had the inside completely renovated; had the Italian marbles, tiles brought from abroad. Did I hear that he had an old fashioned marble basin put in the bathroom, or did I imagine it? I can't recall.

Rabia gave birth to her child in that house. She welcomed her father there.

And then?

I hear explosions. I have been lost in thoughts about the past so much that I am startled by these explosions and holding onto a tree close to me. I am standing there like that. Just then glitters, stars are pouring into the darkness.

---

* Leader of the Muslim congregation.

On the other shore, on the roof of the big concrete hotel, they are shooting fireworks towards the sea. Now all weddings, birthdays, football matches are celebrated like this; a noisy flood of light covers those days when the real bombs kept exploding, took a few lives at every corner. And now, you see... The bombs of light are exploding one after another, first flying in the darkness without being seen and breaking into pieces there, dividing into lit bundles, pouring down in the form of stars and melting on the water. By the sea, those at the house of Karagöz are screaming with joy as if they want to catch this rain of light before it disappears into the water. Some from the boat are throwing their drinking glasses at the crystals breaking in the sky. Many stars are shooting across the sky. At this point where I have been standing and waiting, a voice whispers to my ears that every shooting star represents a life, but my eyes do not see anything to bear out what is whispered: The shooting stars are not in fact pouring from the roof of the universe; they are the shooting stars of non-existent lives. At the dinner party I attended, the conversation was loose and detached. The only clear thing was that nobody wanted to leave Rabia in peace: How can one leave such a husband, why would one return? What is this, if not ingratitude?/Such things were meant to be said. Was it my friend who was married to a Frenchman, yes it was she, who finally declared a full sentence: "Osman was wonderful!'" Those who heard this, while looking at their husbands with reproach, must have had things echoing within them such as: Of course he was wonderful! He had given up everything to marry Rabia, he had been circumcised, had memorized the Koran...

An oil tanker far away. Glides downwards almost scanning the Anatolian shores. Drifts slowly. More than half of its hull sunken in the sea. Must be quite a loaded tanker. Have mercy; hope there's not another accident! Hope the Bosphorus waters are not inflamed again! Such fires do not resemble, of course, the burning of Suad and Necip for each other for a whole summer, the burning of an Italian music teacher of Spanish origin for Rabia for her mysterious voice, secretive glances. The only happy ending here is that the Bosphorus has not been blown up, that the city is not left under ashes... But it is not comprehensible that all these years the Rabia-Italian Osman union was left under the ashes. As if that long adventure had never happened.

The tanker is blowing its foghorn. To this, the ship's flashing searchlight is added. One of the coast guard boals, away from the tanker, returning with the rush of a nutshell fallen on the sea, after making a frightened and trembling round, goes quickly away from the monster. The searchlight is continually flashing. Light spots also flashing in my eyes. The yellow, green, red spots spreading into the darkness of my inner self.

My head is spinning; I stagger. I hinge on the edge of one of the shore benches. In the fog. Rabia and all the people of the town with the fly-filled grocery, are already in the fog. Suad, looking at the men on the sea from the window of the waterfront house is in the fog. The light spots flashing from time to time in the darkness make everything both existent and non-existent. One place is now bright and now sinks into darkness. The past, just when I say I've captured it, caught it, slides away through my fingers. Like that neighborhood, that neighborhood's master of satire and the East-West marriage, both exist and do not exist.

Well to me, wasn't Rabia's life and all the adventure tied to her already a novel whose plot was forced obviously? The lives were always being written, ruined. built again, scattered again by an invisible hand. At one moment, Rabia's deep resonating, mysterious voice from her childhood is becoming more and more melancholic, developing a style of her own, 'her singing a classical and Arabic' mixture; at another moment, she sings whatever she is asked to sing in the bureaucrat's house she has been under the protection, does what she's expected to do, always withdraws herself, cannot ever be herself, cannot fulfill herself.

Rabia... The untouched, pure soul.

So she was described. The converted Osman was to solve her mystery. Lines to be written on a clean, white paper by the hand of a foreign man... Now I think, how passive, how feminine our macho neighborhood was.

These actually were the things that passed through my mind at the dinner. That Rabia already did not have a life of her own, that she was the taken, not the taker... If I had expressed what was on my mind, I would have been scorned: Who is her own self anyway? Then it would be underlined boldly: Who has her own life anyway?

But then, why do they talk about the history that people make themselves? "Who has her own life anyway?"

I am aware of the sigh, a kind of hurt feeling in this statement. Of the rebellion hidden under the hurt, even of the threat. Because, the question is my question anyhow. The answer is mine too. This is the tone of my inner voice. At the same time, this tone is evidence of my genuineness as much as the stars falling down with the fireworks are evidence of the falling lives of those who once lived.

Another one of the floating restaurants that resemble the Karagöz house in the dream screen is passing very close to this shore, protecting itself from the oil tanker. The lights of the boat that are much more colorful, brighter than the previous one, dazzle me. Suddenly, hinging on a bench, I am surrounded by a halo kneaded of light and sound. While I turn my back to the sea, my face to the darkness of the trees, I feel that l hear a laugh. No, probably I think so because of the dust of light I have fallen into.

I come to with a start. Just when I am about to get up, I hear the same laugh, but this time more clearly. I look at the darkness more carefully. l must have been dazzled by the intense brightness a while ago. I wasn't aware of the ghost-like shadow sitting, swaying on the other edge of the bench where I sat. A second darkness out in the darkness! A big jellyfish: Shapeless, faceless, expressionless black-blue mass.

Rabia has returned, they said...

It laughs.

The black mass swinging gently right next to me. This laugh comes from it!

Far away, the lights of a waterside coffeehouse. I must get up. I must get away from here. Am I scared?

Of this shapeless, expressionless, black-blue mass dragging me into its well or of that biting laugh?

This laugh is loaded with a little mockery, a lot of resentment. No, it's rather a laugh reverberating with insolence...

I start to get up quietly. But it is as if the same mass is holding me by my arm. The name spontaneously pouring out of my lips: Rabia?..

It's me of course. It's me, God willing...

This voice reverberates in the darkness, a little shamelessly.

I pretend not to hear. I walk towards the lit coffee-house. The black shadow also stood up and is following me. Maybe I am wrong. Since I heard them say "Rabia has returned," I am full of the dreams of the old neighborhood, of the lives there. Otherwise, where would a Rabia, who had become a thing of the past for so long, come from now? I must quicken my step. But the shadow that is following me, holding me by my arm is not leaving me. The fingers grab my wrist more tightly. I don't see,. I only feel. I also hear: You will listen, I am here you see, don't run away, it says.

Even if it says that it is Rabia, this voice loaded with metallic tones cannot be Rabia's. These kinds of words cannot come out from her lips with so much insolence, even with a kind of vulgarity.

I turn quickly. Why should I run, I want to say. Then, beside me, I see that the black-blue shadow, which was continuously following me, is ripping apart. A window as wide as a big leaf opening to darkness. Through this opening only a pair of eyes are looking. The once deep looking, mysterious eyes are throwing poisonous arrows into the night. This, I sense deep down. The hand that caught my wrist makes me stop with a rough move. Its voice, reverberating like a whistle in the Bosphorus breeze, echoes:

I returned, hah, I returned? Where have I gone? I haven't gone anywhere. I have always been here. At the place I was pushed around. I was here when the piano teacher was stomping on my patience, taking advantage of my loneliness, my lack of support. I was here waiting for him quietly behind closed doors, closed curtains, at the times he went to balls, concerts with you and putting his feet in hot water upon his return, starching his shirt collars...

The glitter, the mother-of-pearl of the love epics we know had long since fallen off. The marriage of Rabia and Osman was going to live in novels, regardless. I realized with a little sorrow that I was not surprised by what it told me. The one beside me still goes on:

You thought that Osman the infidel really fell in love with me! It wasonly a rumor that my heart, too, beat with excitement when I saw him. God is my witness, what I knew from the beginning is that his only love, only desire is to be able to mold someone in the way he wants. What an arrogant man!.. All he wants is to make sculptures out of material that can be shaped easily.

If you knew since the beginning, then why?.. I attempted to interrupt, it did not even listen! Raised its voice a little more, lined up words one after another like verses memorized from the book:

He was in love, blah blah blah!.. Do I believe in such things? What on earth my mother got from her love that I should get anything from some foreign Osman's? This I know, this I say, the only thing he wants is obedience... People in his place, his country had become very rebellious, very uncontrollable in the name of freedom. Especially his ma'! How can this man of ours manage, shape those tough, aggressive people as he wishes? Nobody in the neighborhood could realize this, nobody!.. Grandpa Vehbi[9] Hah hah! Let go with that old peace dove for God's sake... His nest is only good for singing long and sweet, on others' roofs and chimneys.

A little while ago I almost believed this black shadow was Rabia. But, I completely got away from this thought as she chattered nonstop, in a manner refusing to listen. How could she talk like that even about kindhearted Grandpa Vehbi to whom she owed everything she had? No, this is not Rabia. Should I test it? Somehow I break in and ask: You were not so talkative in the past, Rabia?

Now, I was going to say, you are like an old trunk whose lock is broken with everything inside spilled out, and I supposedly was going to lighten the air with a joke, but such a degrading sparkle burned in the gaze opening to the darkness that I understood it was impossible to carry a dialogue in this situation. The shadow, on the other hand, goes on continuously: You see, it says, you see, only one good came of the matchmakers, marriage performers, and those saying amen to all. My patience came to an end while I was being stomped on, my soul and body were shaped and reshaped without anyone asking me. My tongue was untied, thank God! Was it I who reached and look, think about it! Wasn't it me, who was the wanted and the taken?

Just at this moment the biggest, the most ostentatious of the Karagoz houses is passing across the sea. People, not minding the cool weather, in a tumult, a clamor, are applauding from the deck to the shore, some of them are dancing with joy; even before I arrive at the Bosphorus village coffeehouse everything is shouting at me that I won't be able to see again, either the solitude of this place, that I like, or its tranquility which allows one to think even in winter time.

In this tumult, there occurred a subtle breaking in the voice of the shadow beside me. It murmured something I couldn't understand well. Did it say, my son is there too, among them, just to spite me, or did I think it said so? Supposedly, she, too, just to spite them, was covering herself with darkness. That I heard very clearly. Rabia has returned...

I entered the village coffeehouse, ordered a cup of tea.

How many times have I walked through the night together with the night, like this?

Defend My Love You Defend

There were two of them.
They came with a bucket of paint.
They painted over in gray
The many colored wall under acacias
And they left.

Everything wears out quickly. Shoes, curtains, buildings, streets and love affairs. Everything is consumed in no time.

I thought nobody cared about the acacia trees anymore. They seemed more alive and everlasting as remembered in an old song than in real life. However, on the east side of the city the low buildings on a very narrow street still protected them. As did the pale autumn sun that came after the rains. But the nights were cool; they made the dusty green leaves fade. And all autumn long, the leaves kept falling on my mother's lovebirds.

When they passed by our street we felt more cheerful and almost smiled. They didn't hold hands. They didn't put their arms around each other. But, just the same, to us, they always seemed as though they were locked in an embrace. My mother called them 'The lovebirds'. When she said, "My lovebirds are passing by!" what she really meant was, "What's happened to you? You're so gloomy." My husband of a few years would think of our tattered love and smile dejectedly. I'd swear to make a fresh start. And every time they passed by the street I almost felt as though we were rejuvenated. Both my husband and I tried to dispel our deep-seated gloom and keep our love, frayed, from drifting further away out of our will. As we rinsed the bitter taste from our mouths we were eager to give a new zest to our life.

Their hair was always covered with leaves. Pale months and days glided and fell off their bodies like sequins; and they became more beautiful as their steps rustled the fallen leaves. I even believed that they had

come from a faraway place to bring joy at a time when loveliness has been forgotten.

The girl's face was delicate and clear. Her forehead shone with the pride of her love. And the young man carried a little live bird inside his ribcage. They used to talk very little. They appreciated their silence. They made you think they would never do anything rashly. Each time they passed they stopped to sit on that wall under the acacias. From summer through winter the lacy patterns of the branches and leaves reflected on their faces kept changing. But the childish seriousness that came upon them, as they did not waste words in a hurry, and the many-hued pink glow flushing their cheeks never changed. This was so appropriate for their tender youth. Their love seemed to be beyond any apprehension about the future. Anxiety did not seem to have any hold on them.

For months they passed by our narrow street. They sat on that wall many, many times. They talked gently, never arguing, and neither of them ever walked away leaving the other one behind. They nurtured my yearning for a change from the arguments at work, the endless complaints and the dramas forever acted without an audience. Every time I saw them, I would say, if we have to endure until tomorrow, withold yourself dear love.

It was difficult to tell which part of the city they were coming from. They were clothed from head to toe, in their love. Their desires and their freedom were lined up pages.?? So it seemed to me. I kept finding all the evidence to prove my observations. They were the ones who never forgot about the acacias. They always noticed when a baby smiled. They gently picked up a ball rolled under their feet and tossed it back carefully. They never provoked rude behavior from teenagers playing in the street. Anything that interrupted either their silences or their conversations was gently pushed aside, kept away from them. How did they manage to do this in those days when nobody cared for anybody else? I was amazed. And they were the ones to notice the silver glitter of the snow on the bare branches.

My husband said both the young man and the girl were students. I thought they both worked, because they always met on our street at a certain time of the day. My mother swore her lovebirds were also angels. According to her, these two weren't from the city, this country or even this planet. They came from a more perfect world. One day, as my mother was carrying the groceries home, huffing and puffing, she ran into them. They said:

"Let us carry them for you."

My mother right away wanted to make good use of

this encounter to question them about themselves. But tongue-tied, she could only say:

"Thank you my children, thank you. May God bless you and give you all you wish for."

She kept saying: "Oh, they're not only bright and beautiful, but they're also very good kids."

Our gloomy faces puzzled my mother all the more since there were such good people around who could get on in sad and oppressive days as easily as they carried her string shopping bag.

It was the second month of the year. The street was covered with ice. The acacias were bare, their song forgotten. The silvery branches stretched toward a sooty sky. It seemed as if everything was lying in wait. It was an eerie kind of waiting. We didn't know what spring would have in store for us. I couldn't even imagine the acacias' blooming again one day. I kept forgetting to observe their changes. But one thing was certain: As soon as summer arrived there would be the most beautiful wedding for my mother's lovebirds. A wedding that might seem modest from outside, but if one looked carefully from inside, it would be decorated in the colors of a rainbow, with thousands of bright balloons flying all over. This lively and serene love would be the only bright spot on the horizon. The lovebirds were shining like a sign. Many evenings, when I returned from work, I even wanted to run and hug them should I see them passing by. But I wasn't bold enough to do that. Unfortunately, I had learned too well to suppress my spontaneous desires, to keep them hidden under cover. The young couple would soon pass and leave us behind. As for ourselves, we had to be satisfied with the bright sparks they had inspired us. I had to stare at the windows with drawn curtains. Only with the sparks they kindled could I put up with this dull street, the forgotten acacias, and the faces in (on?) which no love ever penetrated. Secretly, but with a dogged perseverance I had to try to find the meaning of life in a love that had neither failed in the past nor would fail in the future and thus would unite the past and the future. Every day as I returned from work my eyes would search for them on the street by that wall under the bare acacia trees.

When the acacias began to bud again my mother's lovebirds no longer appeared in our street. It was as though I had to adjust my eyes to a pitch dark room. I questioned my husband. He told me I was much too preoccupied with them. And my mother with an all-knowing air said:

"Ah, Sooner or later, the lovebirds must fly to their

nest. They couldn't have wandered in the streets forever, could day? They must have gone to their nest."

She seemed half pleased and half sad.

The top of the wall across the street was always deserted now. The acacias lacked something. I had hoped to see them once more. Neither the big flood after the March rains, nor the torrents that carried off all the debris in their way could make me forget the girl and the young man who never appeared in our street again. Now, not only I, but all of us needed that pure love and those clear foreheads. I tried to avoid thinking that bright sign might never have existed. In a place where we had forgotten about love we couldn't possibly stop everything from getting worn-out and being consumed, when the young ones themselves had forsaken love. Perhaps it was all a dream. Only a vain attempt to resurrect our ruined love with a dream.

One day when the acacias were in full bloom, my mother, all worry and flutter, said:

"Ah! You know, our lovebirds didn't have a wedding after all. They couldn't build their nest. Like so many others, those wonderful kids too were taken to jail. Ah, I never expected this!"

I couldn't figure out if my mother had become suspicious of her angels, was worrried about them or disappointed. And my husband in his most reproachful voice said:

"Don't worry, they're close to each other even when they're seperated by great distances. It doesn't matter whether they are together or not.

He turned his face away:

"Some people in the same room are more distant..."

He had summed up his bitter reproach just like that. He had put his signature right there to show how futile were our efforts to restore our love. But he was neither an authority in that matter, nor solely responsible for it; also his rosy view of the prison wards wasn't convincing at all.

However, it is still the dreams that embellish the darkest nights. This time I was fully aware; I had my dreams. I thought that the young man and the girl, in their wards -their foreheads touching the iron bars of the narrow windows- would each look in the other's direction and would smile. Now they would be sharing the moon that was only a sliver in the sky. And the moon made the acacias sharable. Then, I, too smiled. I could lift the fog even a little bit, that had fallen between myself and my husband. I was struggling to have faith. Love kept going on and on. New and lasting loves germinated in dark corners, in narrow places and in difficult times. That strong love, too, would not be punctuated, would not be torn to pieces by hostility. Love would always be a peaceful place, safe from war; it was the only thing that nurtured its endurance with its own forbearance and would not spare itself the effort necessary to withold.

I was waiting for them. I waited for a long time. Another fall came and went. Then winter, then spring again. Twice the acacias bloomed and shed their leaves. I had changed my job. I had left the dramas whose only audience were ourselves. Now, I was trying to produce something durable with my own hands. Thus came the fourth fall, and I saw the young man, at the time when even I had forgotten about him and the young girl.

For quite a while I couldn't believe my eyes. Without the young girl he seemed a totally different person. He hadn't grow taller, nor had he gained weight, no. But the serene smile was gone from his face. His steps were rough. He had let the little bird in his breast escape. That's how I saw it. He came to our street, under the same acacia trees, with other young men, who were about the same age he was three-four years ago; and at an hour when I wouldn't expect to see him there. It was so early. The day was just breaking. No one was passing in the street yet. I had opened my window, I smelled the half-rotted, half-burned odor of the acacia leaves. In the past years, I had tolerated both my husband's inability to fight out rift whose causes were beyond us- and my clumsy struggle to withold, to keep going. Those days were now beyond us. Ahead of us lay many days to live. My mother's lovebirds had multiplied in me. Perhaps that was why I had forgotten the two of them.

Now there, across from me, were four people; all men. And one of them, sure enough, was that young man. I have never seen the others before. In a hurry, they wrote a political slogan, in capital letters in the middle of the wall under the acacias and left. I heard the piercing whistle of the young man I knew, as the stroke of the last letter was made. Was it really him who whistled impatiently and intolerantly to order his friend to hurry up? As I stood by the window amid the smells of the rotted, burnt acacia leaves, this wasn't the question I asked myself though -because the answer was obvious. No matter how much he had changed, he was the same young man, I gave no thought to whether the slogan on the wall was right or wrong, needed or not needed. Only where was the girl? Where was the female of our lovebirds.

No matter what, whichever direction the affair was

going, they should have been doing everything together. This was their promise to the people who had chosen them and their love when they passed by this street in those half-sunny and sunless days. Who had broken this promise? Was it them, the others, the words or death?

I couldn't imagine that the girl had died. That clear, childlike forehead coundn't have fancied death. But one never knows! Death is beyond judgement, like birth. But love is not. No! Not the love that promised life and inspired renewal.

Because of this, I don't at all wish that the last one of the three young people (two boys and a girl) who came, a few days later, by the wall and painted over the slogan in a an ugly yellow, and on top of what was covered wrote just the opposite slogan beginning with "DEATH", has been the girl I knew. Oh, she looked so much like her -the lovebird. I say to myself, but it cannot be her, it just cannot be. -Ah, yes, those aren't just the acacia trees. Anyway, the girl's hair isn't adorned with the acacia leaves. She is passing the brush quickly over the wall -as harshly as the piercing whistle of the young man from whom she once was inseparable. The lacy pattern of the branches doesn't fall on her face. There's no time for that. That forehead, once full of love, is now creased with impatient lines. But, just the same, it is her. She herself with her much used heart quickly worn out in only a few years.

-I could never imagine anything under these acacia trees or over the wall without them. -As long as the acacias existed they too existed. Now, I dread that they might suddenly meet under these same trees by the same wall. The leaves fall one by one, having no time to adorn someone's head. I fear that they too might intermingle with these fallen leaves. They might make each other fall like a leaf by this same wall. Like worn-out love.

Two men came; with a bucket of paint.
They painted over in gray
The many-colored wall under the acacias,
And they left.

I saw it: Nothing but a worn-out wall; love had moved elsewhere.